AF578604

EMOTIONAL INTELLIGENCE SPEAKING ACTIVITIES FOR ESL CLASSROOMS

ExLibric

MARÍA TERESA VICTORIA

EMOTIONAL INTELLIGENCE SPEAKING ACTIVITIES FOR ESL CLASSROOMS

EXLIBRIC
ANTEQUERA 2021

EMOTIONAL INTELLIGENCE SPEAKING ACTIVITIES FOR ESL CLASSROOMS

Diseño de portada: Dpto. de Diseño Gráfico Exlibric

Iª edición

Editado por: ExLibric
c/ Cueva de Viera, 2, Local 3
Centro Negocios CADI
29200 Antequera (Málaga)
Teléfono: 952 70 60 04
Fax: 952 84 55 03
Correo electrónico: exlibric@exlibric.com
Internet: www.exlibric.com

ISBN: 978-84-18912-57-3
Depósito Legal: MA 1136-2021

Nota de la editorial: ExLibric pertenece a Innovación y Cualificación S. L.

MARÍA TERESA VICTORIA

EMOTIONAL INTELLIGENCE SPEAKING ACTIVITIES FOR ESL CLASSROOMS

To my husband, for his encouragement and unconditional support

Research shows that building a sense of community in the classroom is an integral part of creating a positive learning environment. Community building begins on the first day students and teachers come together. It is here that social and emotional learning can be integrated into classroom life. Here, social emotional learning is seen not as an add-on for the teacher but the way that relationships, routines, and procedures are established so everyone feels cared for, respected and valued.

Theory into Practice by Jaqueline A. Norris.

Index

Prologue

I am very lucky to enjoy my work and also learn a lot from the people I work with. For more than ten years I have had the privilege of doing research and teaching at the University of Málaga Programa de Inteligencia Emocional Plena (PINEP - UMA). The Emotional Intelligence Program is developed by accredited professionals such as Natalia Ramos, Olivia Recondo or Liliana Salcido among others.

My most recent years have been enthusiastically devoted to working closely and intensely with hundreds of teachers at Teachers Training Centres (CEPs) and I can assure the vast majority of teachers are exceptional for the engagement, passion and dedication they put into their profession.

Their work does not end once their university studies have been completed, neither when they have achieved a permanent teaching position at Junta de Andalucía governmental schools nor even in their dedication in the classrooms on a daily basis. They actually believe in long-life learning, as a matter of fact, so their work goes beyond already demanding professions into further learning and training, always showing great desire to excel.

Out of love for what they do and how they do it, they want to self-develop and excel at transmitting knowledge, connecting with their students and cultivating their love for the profession itself. It is not otherwise understood that once their workday is over and after spending their personal time on preparing lessons, materials or countless proposals to connect more and better with their students, they dedicate even more time and effort to continue their training, expanding their knowledge and opening up to what innovative proposals CEPs may offer each year.

It was within this group of people who love their work for what it is and for what it can become that I met María Teresa Roura in 2018 when Emotional Intelligence and Mindfulness training courses were organised by Carmen Caparrós at the CEP Marbella-Coín.

Ms Caparrós, to whom we are all appreciative for her professional, trustworthy and enthusiastic attitude, is also a great believer in the importance of Education in society.

During the CEP Marbella-Coín training, María Teresa was already showing signs of being wide open to working on something new. Above all, she seemed well prepared to getting personally involved in the training, which is fundamental when we talk about emotional work.

Just as no one can learn to ride a bicycle only by reading a manual, feeling our emotions and reading about emotions does not necessarily mean that we know how to manage them. Even more so in an efficient manner. María Teresa put all her effort into cultivating, experimenting, working both in a personal and professional level, and sharing what she had learned during the experiential training practice of the PINEP.

Needless to say, for the acquisition of emotional competences to really become more skilful they must travel from a merely cognitive field to a more experiential ground involving changes in those attitudes, habits and concepts that guided us in our personal and professional life before.

María Teresa took a step further wanting to excel for her own improvement and for the students with whom she worked on a daily basis, and we then had the pleasure of sharing time and knowledge yet again during the postgraduate studies in Mindfulness that were completed at the University of Málaga in 2020.

I supervised her final master's work (TFM) when I could give record of all the great effort, dedication and love she showed during the acquisition of competences, resources and experiences, as well as her putting into practice new knowledge of emotional management and Mindfulness. This book along with her blog are the result of all those years of perseverance and dedication to such a rewarding discipline as Education.

Finally, I would like to say that sometimes out of routine, personal problems or other reasons, we forget that bonding is the most important when working with human beings. The effective management of emotions is undoubtedly linked to the acquisition of knowledge, skills and aptitudes in the field of Education in general and foreign language learning processes in particular. We currently live in a very demanding society where everything is expected instantly and sooner done than said. In this context, anxiety can become our students' worst enemy, hence the importance that María Teresa Roura attributes to positive learning climates in the classroom with a sense of mutual respect, belonging and significance.

There are many resources and tools we can have at our disposal nowadays to improve our work as professionals but not so many, though, to improve personal competences. Namely the acquisition of emotional skills or an attitude of acceptance, trust or patience, which the practice of Mindfulness can develop.

This book can be a great resource to enrich the curriculum by adding to the most academic classes a breath of fresh air and gain momentum reminding ourselves of what first motivated us to devote our lives to Educational purposes. The varied proposals in this manuscript can be a great starting point to close bond with our students and provide tools that they might need in their day-to-day life.

Especially we would like to remind students that together with the acquisition of knowledge there are very fundamental things in life such as to raise awareness of our own interests whilst we recognise and defend also the interests of those who surround us.

Professor Oliver Jiménez. Psychologist.
(Málaga, Spain)

Introduction

After thirty years experience as an English teacher I am delighted to share with colleagues from all over the world these 40 group dynamics that have worked well during the days I have had the pleasure of working with ESL students. I truly hope the activities are found useful to complement your lesson plans (resource material can be downloaded from www.mindfulenglish.net).

There is a last set of activities which are kept separately as they were created to suit lockdown lessons during the coronavirus pandemic. These activities are the most special as when I look back I seem to remember my students expressions of worry and concern about the times we were living. My whole intention at waking up every morning was to generate as much connection as possible with them through the videoconference rooms, stay connected and try and forget for two hours that we actually were locked in at home for the rest of the day, week, month... I do remember putting all our heart and efforts into it.

The activities do not follow any other than an alphabetical order. They are not organised by topic, level or skill. I do not normally put lesson plans in a box but rather try and be creative and open, have an outline of what I would like to do and how, then get the feeling of the students in the classroom and decide from there.

Most activities can possibly be adapted to different levels or may inspire you to originally recreate your own for your groups.

Ei FOR ESL CLASSROOMS

1. All ears

"It is a huge welcoming gesture of kindness and hospitality to sit and listen"

For a speaking activity to work well a good "active" Listener is required. Take, for instance, group discussions, trialogues or dialogues. It is the case that sometimes the person you are talking to is, as a matter of fact, not listening. Therefore you cannot expect to get engaged in a conversation then, or follow instructions, receive the right answer to your question or the appropriate comment to your statements.

Closing up our Masters studies at the University of Málaga [February 2019] the importance of opening up conversation in silence to just listen to your partner was pointed out to all participants. As professor Jose María Doria put it himself *"It is a huge welcoming gesture of kindness and hospitality to sit and listen"*. The Emotional Intelligence group dynamics suggested then were to sit quietly for five minutes in small groups of three and pay full attention to your partner. The instructions were to Listen only and not Think of what to say next. Just stay there in silence and observe and welcome their words.

For five minutes one, then the other, then yourself. The experience was phenomenal as we realised how much one misses in conversation when not paying full attention. It shows a conversation can actually flow naturally when you engage into it, connect and respond instead of reacting or over reacting.

My invitation is to practice this exercise first before delivering dialogues to begin with, then trialogues. Once the procedure is understood move finally on to group discussions.

A student who listens carefully and actively is fully prepared to engage in conversation and put into practice all the knowledge obtained by experience or study over the years. As teachers we are accountable for teaching this to our students and for offering encouragement and support so they can achieve their best performance.

SLANT Listening

Listening is actually an art. And in the language classroom it is a must if you wantto have productive and meaningful speaking tasks. So here are excellent tips which teach students to be engaged Listeners paying full attention.

Sit up – Lean in – Acknowledge the speaker – Nod – Track the speaker –Resonate with the experiences

2. Absolute beginners

An ESL teacher for absolute beginners with an emotional intelligence approach will hopefully find this ice-breaker useful when preparing in-class activities for their newly grouped students.

I was wondering what to do in English language with pupils who have not studied English before, how and where to begin if you are not happy with the line "Unit One, page one, exercise one" ... when I came up with this suggestion: pick up some good vocabulary activity that is easy and anyone can just enjoy by very simply Listening and Repeating words!

COLOURS - SHAPES - NUMBERS - LETTERS

So after the typical "Introductions" when everyone knows each other's name, you can ask your group to sit in fours to the count of "One, Two, Three, Four". All "one's" will sit together, all "two's" and so on. Then play the three songs that follow and experience, like explained in the article " Emotional responses to music" [www.mindfulenglish.net] how in fact "music can actually evoke emotions" and in this first session "get people together" as well.

My choice of songs are 1. A million dreams from The Greatest Showman. 2. Me! by Taylor Swift. 3. Back to back by Amy Winehouse

Each group of four, listens to the three YouTube video songs projected on screen. Allow time for them to give opinions on which one they liked best and why. What is their choice of music when they are in the car or at home, etc. Let them talk as much as they like, considering it is their first day at school. Then they can try and determine what is the common factor in them.

The answer is they all are colour-related songs: the first one sung by the artist Pink, the second one displaying an array of colours of the rainbow, the third one with naming the colour in it.

When you think it is appropriate project the Vocabulary Sheet for Colours and hand out coloured pieces of paper at random. Ask the students to Listen and Repeat to the correct pronunciation of The colours of the rainbow. Try to remember how to pronounce their coloured piece of paper. Then write on their piece of paper their name, number and colour. Like this: Peter – two – blue. Finally ask them to tell the other students in their group what their name is, which number group they belong to, and what colour their piece of paper is, for instance, "My name is Peter. I am number Two. I am blue". At the end of the lesson they can pin up their papers on the noticeboard as a memento of their first day at school.

IF YOU HAVE TIME:

You can hand out *shaped* pieces of colour paper as an add-on piece of vocabulary, as follows, my name is Peter, my number is two, I am a blue triangle.

FOR LONGER SESSIONS:

You may like to play The Alphabet song!. It makes it all nice and lively to spread out at random, cut-out letters, or perhaps ask for a volunteer to hand the letters out to their classmates as they are getting in first of all, and then at one point, repeat the sounds of the Alphabet by having each student call out loud their letters one at a time. The effect is very dynamic when you hear the voices of the students from different spots in the classroom like a ping pong ball bouncing from one to another.

You can close up this first session by picking up some colours of your choice to be spelt slowly and quietly as it is their first time. For example, "red". Ask the students to get up as they hear the sound of the letter written on their cut-out flashcard. Then get them all together somewhere visible where the rest of their classmates can see the whole word that has come up with each one of the letters: R - E - D. And sit back down.

Note that this activity can be used to learn and practice numbers and figures as well!

3. Book-crossing

This is a variation of "Indian secrets" (activity 17 page 63) where we take the opportunity to exchange good reads with classmates during dinner at a favourite British "national food" restaurant. A good activity to close-up the first term, for instance, before school breaks up for Christmas.

The proposal is to bring a book that you have really enjoyed and would like to recommend and give away. The books are placed on the table on arrival and stay there during dinner. At some point during the meal the students recommend their books which naturally opens up never ending topics of conversation. Everybody will leave the place with a new book in their hands.

4. Bring in an object

Once upon a time when I was an English student myself in Jane Austen´s Bath (South West England) we were asked to bring in an artifact to this Multicultural training course where we would mix with interesting students from other European countries. The course objectives being to discuss cultural issues.

Our *"Introduce yourself"* session was presented as a Monologue in which we were to tell our classmates about this object from our countries that we had brought with us. Some time later I used The Artifact activity as a speaking task for my Intermediate to Advanced students in mixed-culture groups.

Invite your students to bring in an object that has a meaning to them because they are representative of something, they have been made by someone special or hide an interesting story. Organise the class in small groups of three or four students that will take turns to present their objects and explain why they brought it in today. Every student will speak for about three minutes allowing extra time between one and another for follow-up talk if needed.

The engagement in this activity is enormous as not only are the students sharing fascinating stories of the objects but also connecting bits of their more personal bubbles to the open classroom, which always provides "food for talk" when it comes to something one is really fond of. It is also perfect to enlarge vocabulary lists of descriptive words, expressions and grammar usage.

5. Chain of affection

After all that work my mind just went totally blank and that was the end of my exam

The times I have heard good hardworking students say this, is innumerable. Which is one of the reasons why I got more and more involved with Emotional intelligence activities in the classroom, and Mindfulness practices as a result of all the research.

To do this activity you might like to have had your students trained gradually before as this might feel "a bit too much" to some. The proposal is to build up a sense of belonging and significance, destress the classroom and generate a warm feeling of security before the exam, in a non-punitive environment.

Place your group up forming two concentric circles and tell them there will be some music played at some time. The students in the inner circle will stay still at all times keeping their eyes closed. When the music is heard the students in the outer circle move to one side (all right or all left) until the music stops. At this point one student in the inner circle will be facing one student in the outer circle. With their eyes wide open now the student in the inner circle will signal "one" or "two" with their fingers, one meaning a hug, two meaning two kisses on both cheeks as the Spanish do.

This exercise can be enhanced by a previous brief Mindfulness practice to help students "arrive" and get rooted to the present moment.

6. Christmas wishes

Here are three practices you can try with your students around Christmas time.

Liar's Club and Christmas tree of wishes

The first one worked really well with my Intermediate blended-learning group as a complement for our own version of *Liar's Club* (a game based learning activity brilliantly presented and performed by volunteer students, based on an American production by Ralph Andrews where a panel of celebrity guests offered explanations of obscure or unusual objects; contestants attempted to determine which explanation was correct in order to win prizes). We used our own Christmas vocabulary definitions, for instance, two false descriptions of "poinsettia" next to the real one which contestants had to get right before receiving their Christmas gifts.

The Christmas tree of wishes is made up with star-shaped cut-outs of different size and colour, given to students to write their wishes. All wishes are good. And some in particular are excellent for reading out loud, discussing and reflecting upon them!

There is a grammar structure involved here —I wish— which the students not always understand, so the activity, which may seem naive at first, ends up being an extraordinary "memory game" that helps students fix the structure quite well. Some time before the show allow a few minutes for the students to write their sentences on the stars, then get them pinned up on a board somewhere visible in the classroom. Soft Christmas lights can be added around the stars to give the classroom a good background light that makes the *Liar's Club* show look really professional.

This third activity adapted for ESL students from Emotional Intelligence training courses was organised during the run-up to Christmas in the beginners group. The Advent Calendar is a non-complicated activity that can complement your lessons as a vocabulary revision and consolidation unit. To build up a vocabulary Advent Calendar we displayed images representing the objects in the textbook Vocabulary bank under a real chocolate advent calendar, and provided a box with "Christmas wishes" tags. The Advent Calendar (with photos and tags available) is put on display where every one can see. Every day a volunteer comes to the Advent Calendar and writes a sentence on the tag before it gets pinned around the Advent Calendar, for example, *all I want for Christmas is a mobile phone.* Then they take the chocolate hidden under the numbered cardboard windows in the calendar.

Encourage students to read out loud the dates on the calendar for pronunciation practice before they eat their chocolates!. The result is quite spectacular as the tags will grow in number day after day and will surprise everyone that gets closer to read wishes like "a wallet" but also "health", or "happiness" and "peace".

All I want for Christmas

7. Circles

Rather than an activity itself "Circles" presents an attitude in the classroom. My educational philosophy is based on mutual respect on a teacher- students basis and on a student-student basis as well. The teacher that acts as the person guiding the rest of the group to learn a foreign language and a diversity of cultural issues has my total admiration.

How this shows in the classroom begins with the position everyone takes in the group. I always ask my students to get used to sitting in a circle where they can feel equal and comfortable, to learn, make mistakes, or ask a "silly" question, which will definitely have an answer.

The circle is powerful for several reasons:

- no physical barriers interfere
- everyone faces one another
- students can make eye contact
- everybody feels on the same level
- positive atmosphere stays within the circle

Rather than students "assigning" seats to themselves and/ or their favourite classmates thus keeping closed and fixed mini circles within the group, I much more prefer moving them around regularly so they learn how to cooperate and work together in a respectful and helpful manner. It upsets me to hear students feel left out by others. I find it utterly disrespectful.

Particularly I like to have students sit in circles during Monologues and Dialogues as everyone has the chance to watch their classmates, and give opinions and encouragement in a non-judgmental environment. The feeling of belonging and significance makes sense here.

8. Emotional response

Music can really evoke emotions. You can actually change your students mood by just playing the right music. Perhaps something lively for after lunch lessons or end- of-day sessions. Or maybe some easy- listening after recess for younger pupils.

I like to play music for a "breath of fresh air" after grammar activities which are normally the hardest, or sometimes after intensive reading comprehension exercises. I would recommend that you have a playlist handy. You can do this by choosing your best soundtrack or preferably ask the students which is their favourite "song of the moment" or their favourite "song of all time". They feel more connected when it is a song of their choice but make sure they are present the day you play their song!. Also they can add to the listening task a little bit of conversation practice by telling their classmates more about the song (why they picked it up, what they like about it -lyrics, music, story, any particular piece- or something about the singer, the songwriter, etc).

What I normally do is ask the group during the first weeks to send me a link to their favourite songs in YouTube. Then take the time slowly and patiently to download the songs, label them with their names on it, and keep them in a safe place ready to use anytime!

You don't necessarily need to make much preparation in advance. Just play the video *impromptu* and use the songs as fillers in-between tasks. Songs can be extraordinary listening tasks to learn the new vocabulary and expressions on the video clip, or just as a listening for pleasure exercise as some videos are real masterpieces! Like Perfect by Ed Sheeran, which a student suggested and everybody loved. Turn the lights off and the volume up for greater impact!

One other good musical alternative exercise is a Storytelling mediation activity where students are asked to pick up one song and do some research about the storybehind the song, like the iconic The Bodyguard's soundtrack I will always love you which was originally written by Dolly Parton about the end of a professional career.

9. Elevenses

When I was at college I used to spend marvellous summers in the UK, the country I fell in love with when I was learning English. Among the million things I liked to experiment to become more British than The British, "Elevenses with Granny" was one of my favourites. At approximately 11 am we would pop up into the local farm for the best scones you can dream of, a cup of English breakfast tea or two, and a nice chat.

I don't think many people know it was the Duchess of Bedford, Anna Russell, who started this tradition during the 20th century. She liked her tea and snacks!

I like to introduce this activity in class as an ice-breaker during the first weeks of a new course. As a get-to-know-each-other activity in a "relaxed" atmosphere. Everyone is asked to bring some snacks, biscuits or cookies, and small sandwiches which are nicely placed on a big table. And the kettle goes on...as they do!

You can use previously prepared PROMPTs that the students can hold on to if they are lacking ideas, or hand-out STARs where they would write five words about themselves for discussion, for example, "two, Hitchin, Mindfulness, Northern lights and home".

They will then make questions to each other about these words or explain what they mean to them. Before or after or during "Tea and a nice chat". As a teacher you would be a participant as well (students normally like to hear about your life) and, no need to say, you will always be available too for questions concerning new vocabulary or expressions, pronunciation problems, etc.

I find this is an easy way to distress the classroom and get students to talk in a relaxed, non-punitive, nonjudgmental environment which is when they normally learn best. Also remember "Experiential stays!".

10. 48:1

This is a multidisciplinary linguistic mediation task for C1 students. The activity aims at commemorating International Women's Day and is presented in two different sessions: task a "48:1" as preparation to better understand the historical events before completing task b, no. 32 "woman to woman", on March 8th. This lesson plan is based on Netflix The Crown S4:E8.

I would like to introduce this lesson plan as a snapshot of intense confrontation between relevant women in History to finally highlight the qualities of good female leaders in task no. 32 "woman to woman".

BEFORE THE LESSON

Some time before March 8th students are invited to (1) watch the whole episode in original version at home first of all and just enjoy! Then (2) do some research [links available in www.mindfulenglish.net] on the political context being **"the conflict"** drawn from the **infamous 1986 article** that suggested the Queen had broken protocol and vocalized disappointment with Thatcher's policies. Students are then asked to (3) watch the episode again and take notes. Finally (4) provide examples of possible **fakeness** on the historical events as they are presented on the Netflix tv show.

DURING THE LESSON

In-class **"round table"** on March 8th when the students meet and talk to discuss in small groups the origin of the conflict, its consequences and the resolution.

FOLLOW-UP MEDIATION TASK

Imagine you are a **professor of History** at the University of Málaga and need to prepare a video lesson for your students, explaining this chapter of British politics. Just for practice first of all, deliver your talk before your classmates following these guidelines: write out a draft of your talk, outline your talk from your draft, decide on props and visuals, answer questions carefully, get feedback.

Unprecedented rift

It all begins [Sequence one 08:36 - 09:26] when the Palace Press Secretary is informed of The Queen's frustration at Margaret Thatcher's refusal to back **sanctions** against the Apartheid regime in South Africa, and it is decided after several fail attempts at signing a statement that a word needs to be brought up to replace any reference to "sanctions". The women's differences escalate into irretrievable damage when allegedly HM expresses her political views in public despite the **unbreakable code of silence** between the two Houses.

Queen "dismayed" by "uncaring" Thatcher

For better understanding of the actual context it is recommended that the following scenes are watched with particular interest [preferably with English subtitles for ESL students]. Needless to say, the Netflix series is drama and the dialogues on screen require to be taken with a pinch of salt. Enjoy, and always double-check for true facts!

Sequence two [10:45 - 11:40] Prime Minister's views on the Commonwealth.

Sequence three [14:30 - 15:15] Queen's views on the Commonwealth.

Sequence four [15:45 - 19:07] The two women discussing South Africa.

Sequence five [27:50 - 30:45] Press Secretary's suggestion of a sign of affection from The Sovereign.

Sequence six [34:20 - 35:05] "Queen dismayed by uncaring Thatcher" retold by husbands at breakfast tables.

Sequence seven [37:10 - 42:33] "The" audience after 164 cordial audiences of mutual respect.

Sequence eight [45:35 - 48:30] Consequences of the story's denial.

Please note the same episode can be treated as a Literature and Language Usage activity as well [see activity no. 22 *Mors tua, vita mea*] as it describes Michael Shea's journey from Palace Press Secretary to author of political thrillers.

11. Give thanks and eat pie

Most students will have heard of Thanksgiving and most probably watched movies related to this celebration. They would know about eating turkey and the traditional pumpkin pie.

As they do in Canada and USA, the second Monday of October or the fourth Thursday of November may be a good time in your calendar for this Thanksgiving activity. The proposal is based on the original idea of "Giving thanks".

I like to begin with brainstorm activities like (a) asking students how many English expressions they can use to say Thank you or to respond to Thank you's, (b) listening carefully to what they know about the celebrations, (c) giving examples of things they are thankful for, (d) sharing whether they have moments in their lives or during the day when they say Thank you for a special something that they have received.

Then slowly and gradually get the writing activity introduced by saying they will be asked to write a Thank you note (examples are provided).They are going to watch the videoclip from the movie Mamma Mia! "Thank you for the music" by Amanda Seyfried, and imagine they are that person who walks toward the yellow letter box in the film and puts their envelope in it.

Before they begin the activity or even at the beginning of the lesson you might like to do a simple Mindfulness practice consisting of just sitting still for three minutes, focusing on their breathing and visualising a time when they felt thankful, what they were thankful for, if somebody was involved, or did they just feel thankful for something less specific, more general? Etc.

Then play the video and invite students to recall that moment when they felt thankful, before they begin to write their notes. Allow some time after the music for them to put down some ideas and begin writing (at this stage it is an individual task).When they have finished, they can share their experiences in small groups. Someone might even like to share with the big group. To top up this Thanksgiving activity why not offering some pumpkin pie before they go!

For more engaged students you might like to propose a follow-up activity to do at home "A letter of gratitude" (below). Please contact me for some emotional intelligence strategies for the ESL classroom which I would be delighted to share if you find this task a bit daring.

A letter of gratitude

Write a Thank you letter to a person who, at this moment, is not your friend and with whom you have had some serious conflict, disagreement or misunderstanding.

Write paying full attention to the process of writing a brief letter of gratitude to that person. You can thank him/her for what you want. When you are writing, try to do it without judging the task, or yourself, or that person, or what you are writing. And if you do start to judge, accept what you think and feel but do not get involved in it. "Drop" those thoughts and feelings and continue with your thank you letter.

Focus on the words that come up and try not to think about the final result. Remember that it is not necessary that this letter reaches its recipient, so simply try to express what you feel, without any censorship. Allow your conscious breathing to accompany your writing at all times.

12. Good Things Come in Threes

I am writing this today when many many years have passed since these activities took place in my School Library. The Library was finally opened up on Friday, May 20th 2011 with an interesting major objective: to use the facilities as a Resource Learning Centre [BECREA].

In my position as Deputy Headmistress I was originally commissioned to install this project and promote the students' reading skills. After a 12-month training course organised by CEP Málaga a huge array of possibilities was presented once unveiled the potential of the BECREA. Graded Readers on the other hand, can be exceptional resources for learning foreign languages at any level. So if you want your students to improve their Listening and Pronunciation skills as well, I highly recommend combining reading of actual books with listening to the audio books.

The recommendation is to read the book whilst listening to the audio book version as Reading alone will not help students with their pronunciation in English. Most frequently how a word is written does not correspond with how a word is pronounced. For instance, reading alone will not show students that some words are pronounced the same only spelt differently (like, *heir* and *air)* so if students start introducing audio books they will start to learn these differences and they will start to learn the pronunciation of words. It is a very effective method recommended for students of English at any CEFR level.

I can list here only a few reasons why graded readers are most welcome in ESL classrooms:

- The student is engaged in stories of their favourite genre
- They improve their reading skills
- They can practice pronunciation whilst listening to the audios provided
- They certainly build up their vocabulary
- Their writing skills can get enhanced considerably
- The stories provide great prompt for speaking tasks
- A million collateral topics for discussion come along
- Highlights of the stories can be performed by the students like role- plays or speeches
- You name it...

Here are three favourite graded readers activities:

1. Windows of the Mind
2. Tales of the Supernatural
3. The Importance of Being Earnest

One: windows of the mind

When your advanced students have read "Windows of the Mind" (Cambridge English Readers) whilst listening to the audio, and have completed group discussions, written tasks or role-plays for example, allow some time to enjoy the following Mindfulness practice in the classroom. This activity connected with the senses will not take too long and will create an emotional connection within the group.

A NOSE FOR A STORY

Considering the students seemed to have enjoyed this chapter the most, "A Nose for a Story" has been selected as today's in-class extensive reading activity. In fact, "smell" is understood to be the sense that was first developed in our reptilian brain. One effective way to connect with the present moment thus helping the brain reset, de-stress and renew is through the senses. It has also been proven that bringing awareness to exteroceptive senses and bodily sensations [Mindfulness] can develop our cognitive learning skills and that our abilities to engage in tasks can improve when emotions are involved. The theory of senses and how emotions can be created through sight, hearing, smell, taste and touch is highlighted during this practice.

Present this activity by building up as much excitement and curiosity as possible.

So bring a nice box into the classroom and carefully leave it on the table in the middle of the room. Invite students to stand up close around the table, and brainstorm what they can imagine is in the box. Then open the box slowly and ask them to take one of the contents each [unlabelled perfume bottles] and use adjectives describing their sensations and perceptions as they smell the scents.

As the chapter is about writers you can provide extra material with vocabulary (like "words that describe smells") prior to the task.

When they have taken their time to choose a favourite perfume and are emotionally connected to the activity and their classmates, encourage them to share to whom they would like to present these perfumes and why. For instance, "this perfume would suit my daughter ideally because of its sweet fragrance and its pleasant scent".

The activity can be perfect for the run-up to Christmas

Two: tales of the supernatural

This story from Cambridge English Readers could not be more appropriate for October 31st as a "reading for pleasure" activity.

Prepare the class in advance with artificial candles, and treats scattered all over the desks, which will have been set in a circle where students can face each other. Explain students will be reading passages of their choice out loud, and sharing reasons for their choice. For instance, I have chosen this paragraph from "Irish Rose" because I loved its ending which I found totally unpredictable. While they are reading, a tray with candies and chocolates circulates around for the students to pick treats.

When all students have participated they can choose which of all those passages that have been read made the story most exciting, following pronunciation, intonation and rhythm criteria provided. The best story read will receive a special treat. And if one of your students does face-painting the group picture will certainly look its best!

Here is how the second option is organised:

To prepare for the actual task in-class, divide the students into small groups some time in advance and assign one different chapter for each group to read. To improve pronunciation ask the students to read the story at home whilst listening to the audio book.

On 31st October invite students to sit in mixed groups where every person will have read a different chapter. Students take turns to re- tell the story that they have each read. Some Q&A time can be set after each "Monologue". At the end of the session all kinds of spooky stories with unexpected endings will have been heard in each small group and the contents of the book will have been learnt in the big group.

The "real" meaning of Trick or Treat is learnt during the session

While the students are telling / listening to the "tales of the supernatural" the face- painting stand will be welcoming those who would like to leave the classroom at the end of the session with Halloween symbols created by their make-up artist classmate.

Three: the importance of being earnest

During the BECREA course sessions mentioned above a fascinating post-reading activity named "Literature and the senses" was presented, which caught my attention like a magnet and reads as follows:

The senses can be used as an extraordinary way to bring fiction into reality. Take, for example, this scene from Oscar Wilde's *The Importance of Being Earnest* immediately after the play opens, where Lane and Algernon are telling a cucumber sandwich joke. Algernon has prepared the cucumbers as a treat for his aunt, Lady Bracknell (in the Victorian age, food was used as a sign of respect and hospitality to visitors and also as a form of socializing).

The Importance of Being Earnest Oxford Graded Readers

So what we did was recreate a similar scene in The School Library where a nice tray with cucumber sandwiches was presented for the students. And while they were taking turns to read out loud their favourite paragraphs from the book or most relevant passages in the story we were enjoying the tastes and flavours of the cucumber sandwiches "prepared by Algernon". The effect and the students engagement is quite different from a most common reading comprehension activity without the cucumber sandwiches as you can imagine... and all sorts of questions arise from the "social interaction" about British recipes and chefs, historical characters like Oscar Wilde or travelling destinations like Dublin, in fact, we ended up organising a school trip to Ireland some time later...

15. Heartfulness on Valentine's Day

MAY YOU HAVE A NICE DAY

On Valentine's Day we are all invited to show Love of any kind really, don't you agree? After all, love is in the air! When I have done this activity in class I have always had a box ready with red and white heart-shaped cut-outs on a nice tray.

I have asked my students to think of something they would like to tell their beloved today when they get back home, or something they would like to hear from their friends or relatives, and write that on the heart shaped cut-outs. For instance, "may you be healthy" or "may you actually be happy". It only takes a few minutes for the tray to get handed around the students' desks collecting messages that are actually addressed to someone in their mind.

The lesson continues as usual with language activities until a few minutes before we go I remind the students there are heart shaped messages waiting to get picked up. At random, they get theirs and read them out loud if they are happy to share. Try this and see the expressions on their face as they leave the room!

GRATITUDE JAR

I like to use this activity for Valentine's Day too. It doesn't take too long and students learn some grammar rules as well as vocabulary and expressions in a very spontaneous way. First thing in the morning, ask your students to "write on coloured pieces of paper things they are grateful for or thankful for". These can involve their own classmates showing acts of kindness, for instance, "I am grateful to Julius for always being polite" or "I am thankful to Millie for explaining the meaning of 'flabbergasted' to me" or "I am grateful to my teacher for her patience and understanding".

Allow a few minutes for them to think of precious examples they would like to share, and to put their coloured papers into a glass jar (preferably transparent). Leave the jar somewhere visible for the rest of the session, and a few minutes before finish-time ask for a volunteer to open the jar up and slowly and carefully read out loud (anonymous if preferable) everyone's examples of things they are grateful for. The feeling of gratitude and heartfulness will surround you all if you do this activity in a conscious way. Invite them to try the "Gratitude jar" activity with their families... I have a Gratitude jar at home which I enjoy bringing out onto the breakfast table every now and then. I like to get my family read old messages from previous Valentine's. We love listening to them.

16. Hermes

I find "Hermes" a nice and easy way to close up an activity. Like favourite end-of- term dynamics, a lesson or an anecdote. End-of-course positives and negatives, or proposals and suggestions. Also good for New Year's Resolutions, for instance, or vocabulary and expressions activities, learning strategies...just to give you a few examples. Feel free to adapt this activity to your lessons!

PROCEDURE:

Hand out stripes of coloured papers and markers. Ask students to write, for example, the good things about the lesson / term / course on one side and the not-so good things on the other side. When everybody has done so get a volunteer read out loud what they wrote on their piece of paper, staple the ends together and decide whether the person to their right or left goes next. The next person repeats the action, and starts making a chain of coloured papers (as in the illustration above).

This simple exercise does have an impact on all participants, including the teacher, as everybody gets heard (or all opinions are taken into consideration if it is the case). Plus watching the chain grow longer with the students words and thoughts is beautiful too. Finally hang up the chain somewhere visible in the classroom.

17. Indian secrets

Needless to say L2 is spoken from start to finish!

Extracurricular activities can be excellent opportunities for students to learn foreign languages in less formal contexts. It is common practice to organise end-of-course meals or celebrations as close-up out-of-school activities but why not do the same when a new course begins. As a student in Kew Gardens myself (London 1992) we got invited on arrival to a garden party after the first day at the Language School. What happens in these informal meetings is not only that you get to know your classmates during more natural encounters but also you learn what cannot be found in books, for example, expressions like *"You can't have the cake and eat it"* and most interestingly you can learn a lot about British humour. It is all part of the Learning process.

So with Intermediate to Advanced students an evening out can be organised as an outdoor activity at the beginning of a new academic year as well. Our choice of venue for quite a few years were Indian restaurants following the fact that Chicken Tikka Masala is popularly referred to as *"Britain's true national dish"*, and

Curry Houses, as they are also called, are easily found in our area. No preparations needed for this activity in particular. Just enjoy the company and let it be. The students will be learning from the moment they arrive and introduce themselves to then sit at the table, read the menu and order their courses, until they part with a good big picture of their new classmates for the year.

18. It's Christmas time

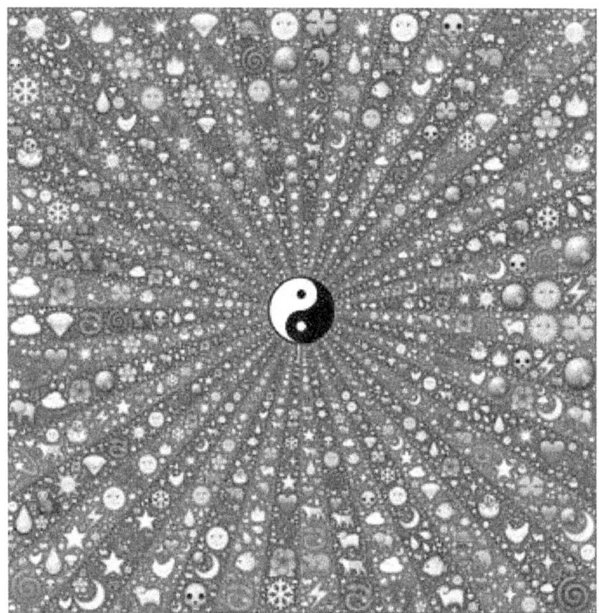

I am sharing here what was once part of the Christmas workshops prepared by both my group and myself. The song chosen for this workshop was *Do they know it's Christmas* by Ban Aid. In 2014 the United Nations had contacted them, saying help was urgently needed to prevent the 2014 Ebola crisis in Western Africa spreading throughout the world.

PROCEDURE:

Introduce the song and some of the events related to it, then tell the students you are going to ask them to please get up and group like in the YouTube video clip. The are invited to sing in turns: altogether, male voices only or female voices only following instructions given with the lyrics. The students will not only improve their full attention to what is happening at the moment, as they will need to know when is their turn, but also experience the feeling of coexistence and connection.

A little interesting note: you don't have to be a great singer to participate in this activity. Projecting your voice may be related to how you connect with your inner self. The more aware and connected you are to do a deep diaphragmatic belly breathing the clearer and easy your voice will come out. Singing out aloud is not needed! Try "whispering" and just connecting to your breathing.

19. Learn by doing

Long experience as a teacher and most importantly as a long-life student, tells me that whatever one learns through practical instances gets registered best. Even more so if it is done collaboratively and with a plus of excitement. Experiential stays.

The activity I'm sharing today is our 25th anniversary trip to London. No need to say language students who are motivated to use their second language outside the classroom learn fast! At work, neighbourhoods, family environments, etc. An outdoor activity whether short or long-distanced is always an excellent opportunity to get exposed to the language in a less formal practice. Relaxed environments where one is "not being assessed or marked" help students produce long speeches and smart conversations. After all, chatting about "life-work balance" over dinner, to give an example, is not the same as discussing the topic in Trialogue based speaking examinations!. The stress factor makes a difference.

I have been a proud witness of outstanding conversations between English students during visits to museums, theatre plays, cities, or countries. Like this end-of-course trip to London described here.

The suggestion is to get the activity done as a class project where everyone is a participant. The students practice their English from beginning to end. From trying to find their own flights on well-known sites to sharing experiences with other passengers on the flight back home.

The proposal is for the teacher to set a calendar to program the activities: (1) get flights asap as fares rise quickly, (2) provide sources for students to choose possible destinations within the city or surrounding areas, (3) give links to social events and entertainment, (4) and to visit hotel websites for prices, facilities, etc, (5) get together to finalise program of activities. And TRUST them.

The pleasure of generating amicable and respectful relationships in your classroom creates an atmosphere of connection and belonging where everyone feels welcome and is well-looked after. Everybody helps to find places or with map reading. Everyone is treated as a free individual who is part of a non-judgemental group. And by doing this ... things flow naturally in a very responsible manner.

The reward is not just to see the students faces of amazement at the musical, or witness their laughters after the "panic attacks" when getting on the wrong line in the tube, or getting back to the hotel to sit and tell stories of the long day gone. The real reward is to be the last one to get out of the plane and find your whole group waiting at the lounge to say Thank you for the trip and a big hug.

When you and your students manage to experience this, it all makes sense. And most important of all, it's all in English!

20. Let's go hybrid

With the new preventive measures for coronavirus pandemic schools, having to wear face-masks may add to the **language barrier to effective communication** in the classroom. But as the saying goes "every cloud has a silver lining", and it looks like the answer is to make the best of technology and go hybrid!

BEFORE YOU WATCH:

I am leaving this song here for you "Everybody is changing" by Keane, to play while the students are making an entrance, coming in and sitting down. Background music is a great help to break the ice.

The proposal is to project your own "presentation video recording" on this first day at "covid schools". So have your MP4 file ready and wait until your students are all settled in the classroom – keeping their regulatory social distance. Then briefly explain you will be coming up on the screen where you will not be wearing your face mask, to introduce yourself and give details of the new course.

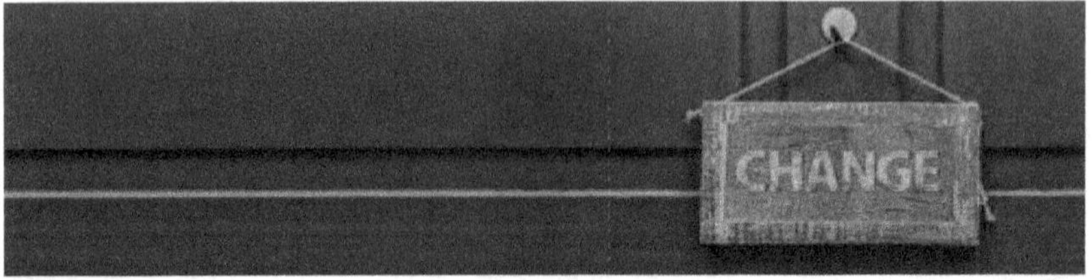

AFTER YOU WATCH:

When students have met the person behind the mask on the screen, open up some Q&A time to discuss lesson plans and materials as well as to ask any curiosity questions that are relevant to the new course or the video, allowing those students following from home to participate.

FOLLOW-UP:

Students prepare a similar speech at home and upload their videos to our virtual classroom. If there is plenty of time they can sit in pairs -social distancing- and start making preparations for their videos as an in- class activity, so leave your mind-map visible on the board for them to brainstorm ideas and create a similar one. Mine was rather simple consisting of the pronoun Me written in the middle of a circle with spikes pointing out at significant words and figures for myself, like 1993 - MSL - multidisciplinary.

They can also write their draft paragraphs as preparation for their speaking task, which will be projected and watched in-class the following day.

VARIATIONS:

With your advanced students why not ask them to watch and enhance the teacher's speech!

- What other expressions could she have used?
- Which synonym would have been a better choice of words?

– How appropriate was her closing up line?
– Or what ideas, reasons or opinions could have been added?

Let's get ready for this new journey!

21. A lucky charm

June 2012 marked the beginning of a new era for students at Official Schools of Languages in Andalucia as new assessment criteria were followed, which also modelled teaching methods in the classrooms and students skills and performances.

In those exam days the students felt more and more pressure as the new procedures for examinations were rather strict and meticulous in an attempt to assure that candidates were sitting identical exams in any school within the Andalusian region: same exam, same timing, same requirements, same certificates. L-o-n-g sessions.

Speaking tests became more specialised in form and content asking students to deliver monologues and dialogues based on the CEFR fourteen general categories for speaking tasks.

The case of B1 students

In those times between 2012 and 2018 I developed an enduring appeal of B1 groups. The reason was to be able to prove whether students leaving A2 in June could actually become proficient students in B1 only one year later. What was proven each year really was how hard promotion was for our B1 students who most times were obliged to take the course once more. And even once again in the event of an illness or change of workplaces as it very sadly was the case of this hardworking person, who became my student at one point. The paradox being his University degree would have no effect before his B1 certificate was issued.

A lucky charm

It was then that this idea was born for my B1 students who had worked really hard all year and were feeling anxious and stressed up in front of exam papers: a few minutes before the exam begins hand out "four leaf clover shamrock" tokens as a symbol of encouragement for the students. Walk around their desks giving one cut-out clover each as you wish best of luck to them all. Slowly and meaningfully. You will see it in their faces... it will show later on in their results.

Another turning point in Legislation occurred in June 2020 with newer skills being introduced, along with newer criteria expanding B1 level into three years instead of one which hopefully be more student "friendly". I couldn't be more in favour of this.

22. Mors tua, vita mea

This activity for advanced ESL students originates in the historical consequences of an unprecedented rift between 10, Downing Street and Buckingham Palace represented in The Crown S4 episode 48:1 (Netflix), which we discussed and studied before in activity no. 10 "48:1".

The passage describes Michael Shea's journey from Palace Press Secretary to author of political thrillers. For **linguists' delight** do not miss the first few minutes [Sequence one 06:06 - 07:18] that give title to the activity, and the reading of proposed texts [28:18] that we will further down deep into.

The proposal is for Language and Literature **lovers** to enjoy the appreciation of one's **choice of words** and to raise awareness on the **impact of Language Usage** in speech. Not to mention, the consequences.

The passage gives a report of this **statement** that needs to be signed between the UK and the 48 member countries of the Commonwealth over whether or not to back **sanctions** against the Apartheid regime in South Africa in 1989. Michael Shea is chosen to provide **the right words** that Margaret Thatcher would not disagree to sign.

The complete episode can be watched in advance so that students fully understand the historical circumstances surrounding the sudden and fatal **turning point** in Michael Shea's career. Then, in class, they can be asked to watch only these small pieces

- Sequence two [19:49 - 20:17] where it all begins
- Sequence three [20:20 - 22:04] PM starts scrutinising the proposals
- Sequence four [22:28 - 23:22] Palace Press Secretary studies alternatives
- Sequence five [37:44 - 37:58] Code of silence between the two Houses

and, in pairs or groups of three, take notes of those words rejected by The Iron Lady as well as the synonyms she is offered each time. Students can provide their own alternative texts too, paying attention in particular to the subtle differences between pairs of words. They can give definitions of a sanction compared to an embargo, for instance.

sneak *yell* *peer*

clutch *giggle*

Turning subtitles on can be a good opportunity to introduce descriptive verbs

Could you possibly rephrase that

Don't you think it would be interesting to ask for volunteers to report the events back to the class? By focusing on mediation techniques, like "paraphrasing" which I find super challenging and the most effective, advice your students to begin their daily practice and rewrite sentences in such a way that the meaning stays the same [365 sentences available in www.mindfulenglish.net].

23. Musical chairs

This activity serves different purposes. Here is a "First day at school" proposal. The same dynamics have been used in my class to revise and check banks of vocabulary and it works very well too. Always an opportunity to liven up tired students or to open up and interact with a different classmate. The shyest don't like it much at first, the most energetic love it. Give it a try!

First day at school

If you want to begin a new course in an unexpected manner keep reading. This was a fun activity for me as a participant in a teachers training course and I thought my students would love it! So this year I used it myself as an ice-breaker. I had my large group dance around musical chairs. My not-so-large group responded to names of fruits which worked well too.

OPTION A: With a large group of students you can simply follow the traditional game. Everybody sits in a circle. Then explain you are going to play some music and when the music stops everyone is to find an empty chair to sit on as quickly as possible. The person left without a chair will give two or three pieces of information about themselves. At random. For instance, "My name is Peter, I hate coffee and my favourite music group is Queen" or "Hi! I am Sophie, my daughter lives in London and my cat's name is Arlo".

Before you play the music remember to always remove one chair. Repeat the sequence over and over again until only one student is left to introduce himself. I can assure you this person will be remembered for the rest of the course!!

As the activity develops you will find that students will already be grouping themselves according to their likes and dislikes, position in the family, or favourite sports for example. "Musical chairs" is very easily followed up by get-to-know-each- other discussions. The activity works well with latest music hits that students can recognise. Some even sing along.

OPTION B: Everybody sits in a circle. Depending on how many students you have name three or four fruits (for example, apple, orange, grapefruit). Students then choose which fruit they want to be for the exercise. If you have 15 students then you will have five oranges, five apples, and five grapefruits in the classroom. For larger groups just add more fruits!

When everybody has picked up a name, remove one chair and explain the procedure to your group. The instructions are the following: the activity begins with everybody walking nicely around the chairs until the teacher calls out the name of a fruit, for example, Apple. When the word "apple" is heard all the students will need to find a chair to sit on as quickly as possible. The student who stands up will give some information about themselves like "I go to the cinema every week and my favourite actor is Rami Malek".

During the second round the student who has introduced herself will then name another fruit, for example, grapefruit. All "the grapefruits" will start walking around the chairs nicely and slowly until the music stops and the grapefruits go and try to sit, except one! This person then will say something about herself, for example, "I am single and I play paddle twice a week" and give the name of another fruit, for example, orange. Then all "the oranges" will start walking around the chairs until the music stops. And so on and so forth.

The students who have had a chance to introduce themselves will remain seated within the circle during the rest of the exercise.

Mistakes are great opportunities to learn

I like to give students a pice of paper before beginning the activity. The word SHAME is written on the paper. They are asked to throw that piece of paper in the bin outside the room before entering the classroom. Then, during lessons throughout the year, every time they feel embarrassed to speak in public or repeat an "awkward" sound I ask them to please remember "no-shame in class" as mistakes are great opportunities to learn!.

Be creative

24. Of foxes and hedgehogs

The virtual bookclub initiative that was born on lockdown March 2020 stands up as a permanent option for advanced students in the present academic year. In these *multidisciplinary* workshops we are reading and listening to stories, discussing collateral issues, and studying historical characters or events in depth. Not until we have all enjoyed these activities, are we actually ready to put it in writing.

What happens is that when writing there is one recurrent message from the participants handing in their tasks: the students who must work on stories retold or summarised find it hard and difficult to simply "start" writing!

Sometimes they have too many ideas, or they have none at all, or they just don't really know how to end up their compositions. At times, they regret not being capable to "recreate scenarios" or "build up characters" as well. They finally admit failing to complete their assignments even more when they are asked to freely write some lines after a given prompt, for instance, "for sale baby shoes never worn".

For sale baby shoes never worn

So I thought what I only just found out on my latest video lessons, first hand from the acknowledged Spanish author Rosa Montero, might actually help students. The starting point for my dear students, is to reflect upon what type of writer they believe they could possibly be first of all. And be creative…

HERE COMES THE TWIST

Creativity has to do with imagination and with letting our inner child free. Imagination is the most natural feature in one child. Children are capable of building up the most amazing stories from nothing.

> *"Creativity is inventing, experimenting, growing, taking risks, breaking rules, making mistakes and having fun", Mary Low Cook*

Unfortunately, as we grow older with commitments and obligations, our inner child gradually vanishes in a world of conventions and control.

To go back to making up stories and being able to create something again we must try and set our inner child free. Let their imagination fly. It is an act of freedom in fact to open up that window and let the magic back in to inspire our inner child to write truths or lies. Stories, tales or fables. Memories, feelings, emotions. You name it.

So I do hope it helps my ESL students sitting in front of blank pages for hours running out of ideas for their written tasks, to read about the following interesting classification of writers which I found the most insightful during Rosa Montero's lectures (organised by CEP Málaga).

What type of writer are you

The awarded Rosa Montero describes all different kinds of writers falling into the types that follow:

1. A hedgehog writer, like Marcel Proust, always writes the same novel, actually going deeper and deeper within the same sort of story over and over again.
2. A fox writer, like Rosa Montero, looks for new horizons always trying to find new ways of saying whatever she wants to put in writing.
3. A flame writer, like Patricia Highsmith, is forever passionate and emotional.
4. A glass writer, like Thomas Bernhard, shows no emotion, and is logical and intellectual.
5. A mammal writer, like Leon Tolstoi, recreates childhood memories, and creates gigantic narrative constructions where we wouldn't miss a few pages should they have not been written.
6. An insect writer, like Franz Kafka, creates rather succinct novels with little embellishment.
7. An amnesiac writer, like Joseph Conrad, makes his characters pop out from nowhere, with very little detailed descriptions.
8. An architect writer, like Vladimir Nabokov, believes in a well-structured masterpiece.
9. A chronological writer, like Iván Turguénev, believes in simplicity at first sight.
10. A torrential writer, like Martin Amis, completes pages and pages unnecessarily.
11. An emaciated writer, like early Rosa Montero, lacks flesh creating scrawny stories.

The invitation is to discuss this with your students and encourage them to show their admiration for either writer/s explaining why they would believe they could be a similar type of writer. Then write.

25. Remote Thanksgiving

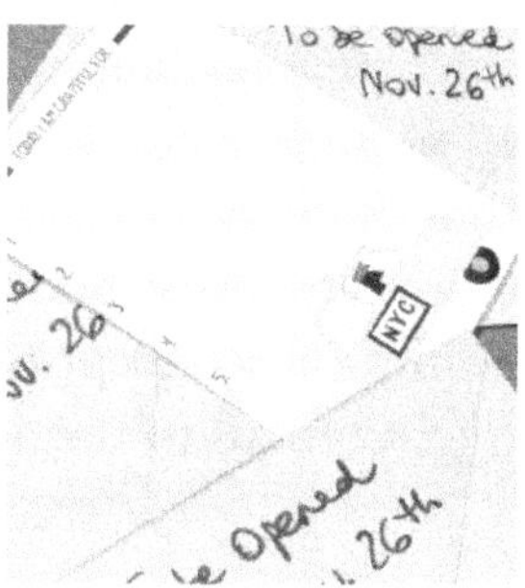

For a Remote Thanksgivings session, let's go vintage.

1. Put "I am grateful for" cards inside your envelopes
2. Up they go into the drop box!
3. Ask your students not to open their letters until the last Thursday of November.
4. Fill in their "I am grateful for" cards.
5. Like, share, comment on social media!

What am I thankful for?
Ask yourself this question regularly.

26. Soft skills

With the update of the CEFR bringing new referential areas like mediation and the rise of a new emerging concept of what it is to be part of a team or what it is to get your ideas across, the four c's have become important skills for the coming years.

The four C's – **collaboration, communication, creativity and critical thinking,** often referred to in Education as Soft skills have been identified by the world economic forum as relevant skills in the 21st century where working scenarios might take the shape of international teams of people having English as a common language.

The first two are transversal skills present across all of this as when we are managing people engaging in emotional intelligence, or when we are problem solving, which is today's proposal for our speaking task for advanced students. The activity is based on

"Urban solutions" from our course textbook Outcomes. I have added a slight extension into the concept of *mediation* and chosen to give an *emotional intelligence* focus to the activity as well.

PROCEDURE:

In pairs students are handed out role cards with problem situations in an imaginary neighbourhood (from Outcomes communicative activities), then asked to imagine they are the person on the card and tell their problem to their classmate. Once everybody has described their problem situation to their partner, this new dimension to the activity gets added by asking the students to ***synthesise and repackage*** their partner's problem situation for the rest of the participants. Students may have to ***adjust the language*** when transferring the information gathered to the group and take ***presentation format*** into account.

The objective is to ***resolve collectively*** a delicate situation related to urban problems. And while doing so I would like to shine a light on the mindful attitude of showing ***empathy*** to the speaker by simply **active listening** to them.

A very simple practice can be to remain quiet for a few seconds before the next person begins to talk... and **breathe...** allowing some time to let the problem settle down a little before we are prepared to hear the next problem. Being ***open*** to the problems on display might support more respectful interactions.

When all problems have been discussed ask one volunteer student to ***summarise*** the solutions they came up with, and discuss whether the solutions met their demands.

Functional language toolkits can be provided as students might find them useful for discussions.

27. Take it personal

Connection before correction

Time is golden, no need to say this. How we manage time is in fact one of the biggest stressors in Life and can cause anxiety even illnesses. Mindfulness can actually help us regulate this. What we do with our time is in fact based on priorities and to devote TIME to students is certainly a priority for this teacher. Specially when it comes to letting students know, learn, and register what they are doing well and what they are not doing so well.

I am not particularly fond of having students check their final marks on online platforms either really, by looking at a "cold" list that someone has uploaded on an empty virtual board. I believe this moment to be one of the most important in the learning process. I certainly like to take it personal as "connection comes before correction" and this key session will transform the rest of the course indeed.

In fact, how you give feedback to your students matters. So in the middle of the school year or during end-of- term lessons, organise your session so that everybody has a chance to go through their summary of assignments and results, or look at their exam papers (with answer keys) and assessment sheets (with the teacher's notes or marks). While they are doing this stay somewhere visible and available for any group curiosities, questions or suggestions. Stay calm, open and receptive as students may come up with good proposals.

After this first stage, invite them to meet you at "the feedback corner" which should be a welcoming place specially prepared to discuss issues concerning their learning process. Take the time, one by one, to help them. With a focus on solutions. Encourage them to do some planning and commitments. Success is sometimes a matter of attitude, concern and resilience.

Talk to them. Explain to them nicely and clearly where they must make the biggest efforts, how they can refresh concepts, where they can find useful materials. Restore their self-esteem if needed, and most importantly encourage them to keep going!

This does take TIME when you have large groups but I can assure you the benefits of this just one session are big. For the students and for the group as a whole. They will leave the room much more aware of their handicaps and also their assets which will change their attitude during lessons afterwards. It is the 80/20 rule!

Mindfulness can help us manage our time

28. Ten for dinner

To celebrate a very unrehearsed Christmas this year, full of improvised moments and impromptu decisions I am sharing this cross-cultural and cross-linguistic mediation task today.

CROSS-LINGUISTIC/CROSS-CULTURAL

In small groups students take different roles to do some research on British customs, *take notes, translate* and *simplify* texts related to Christmas traditions. They will also need to *transform* specific information from *visual* material. In the last stages they will eventually need to discuss options and *show personal reaction* connected to *previous knowledge* on British Christmas essentials.

In order to write your notes you must *understand, select* and *transmit* the most relevant information from the links available on www.mindfulenglish.net to recreate a little British atmosphere for the unexpected guest. Do not forget to adapt the Imperial units of measurement.

SCENARIO 1: Because of the coronavirus pandemic precautionary measures a recently widowed British lady from your grandparents' community will not be able to meet her family this Christmas, as the recommendation is to stay local.Your grandparents have very kindly invited her to join for dinner and have now asked you guys obviously, to do a great deal of the job!

To avoid unwanted misunderstandings the whole family will need reminding that Christmas Dinner will be celebrated on December 25th 2020 - more like "late lunch" time for Spaniards. The hosts will appreciate your help reading through the Christmas recipes [available on www.mindfulenglish.net], telling them roughly how to cook the traditional turkey British style for their guest, and to prepare some snacks in advance.

#stayhome #feelsafe

SCENARIO 2: They have also suggested you all set the table nicely as you spent Christmas in the UK once on a High School language exchange activity. So, said they, "You guys must know it all very well!". Besides, you have been asked to explain how to watch the traditional Queen's Speech at 3pm (English time), which, given the circumstances, apparently can be followed on *streaming* this year.

Good luck in making this unprecedented Christmas Dinner unforgettable!!

29. The Arts

Movies and The Arts in general are long-lasting resources for English learners. Here is a list of movies, representative of emotional intelligence or Mindfulness, on which you may like to base some of your activities. [Links to official trailers and reviews available in www.mindfulenglish.net].

Asking for help: Looking for Eric by Ken Loach

Benefits of Mindfulness: Peaceful warrior by Victor Salva

Connectedness: Legend of Bagger Vance by Robert Redford

The comfort zone: Jack and the Cuckoo-clock heart by Mathias Malzieu and Stéphane Berla

Compassion: The Salt of the Earth by Wim Wenders and Juliano Ribeiro Salgado

Emotional intelligence in politics: Diplomacy by Volker Schlöndorff

Empathy: Jerry Maguire by Cameron Crowe Equanimity: Darkest Hour by Joe Wright

Family life dynamics: The Tree of Life by Terence Malick

Here and now: The Brand New Testament by Jaco Van Dormael

Hope: The Shawshank Redemption by Frank Darabont

Instinct for survival: Life of Pi by And Lee

Letting go: Departures by Yojiro Takita

Maladaptative emotions: Inside Out by Pete Docter

Manipulation: Die Welle by Dennis Gansele

Non-striving: Spring, summer, autumn, winter...and spring by Kim Ki- duk

Non-verbal communication: Wall-E by Andrew Stanton

Self awareness: A Beautiful Mind by Ron Howard Self confidence: Hitch by Andy Tenant

Self esteem: Angel-A by Luc Besson

Self-improvement: The King's Speech by Tom Hooper

The task: the suggested speaking activity is to deliver a Monologue on likes and dislikes in terms of films that you can base on the above. The proposal is for the students to record a monologue and receive feedback from the teacher. The benefits of the students getting recorded are described in my blog (www. mindfulenglish.net). I have two favourite techniques to provide feedback on recorded speaking tasks: one is notes synchronised with videos using videonot.es and the other is to record my own video clip with comments on the task… Students seem to appreciate the latter as more "horizontal".

Share your likes and dislikes in terms of films

30. The Guest House

March 21st "World Poetry Day" is probably the best day for this task. The poem by Rumi has become a constant reference in my every day life describing well the world of emotions. Moment by moment we get visited by emotions that come and go. Being able to observe those emotions, accept them, and regulate them, develops our emotional intelligence skills.

The task: some days before the activity ask your students to find a poem they are fond of and that they would like to bring to the classroom and share with their classmates. It can be a poem written in their mother tongue or in English.

In class, you may want to present the activity by telling them we are going to watch this video as an introduction to the task. Perhaps invite them first to just sit down for three minutes, close their eyes and concentrate on their breathing, disconnect from all the stress of getting into the classroom, finding a parking spot, worrying about homework (not) being done, or welcoming other students before the lesson. Just focus on here and now. Be open to what comes next. And breathe.

After the brief Mindfulness practice, read the poem by Rumi The Guest House (available in www.mindfulenglish.net) for your students and ask them to read their poems out loud to their classmates in small groups and discuss: what the poem is about, why they picked it up, what they know about the writer, what they like about the poem, etc.

Follow-up by brainstorming ideas for poetry writing: do they think anyone can write a poem, or that creativity is something you are born with, are poets driven by "negative" emotions, can poetry skills be learnt, etc. We can explain that creativity may be enhanced by practising Mindfulness as one is more connected to their inner self.

Close up by asking them to try and write a poem in pairs or small groups. One line each. And share their newly-written pieces of art with the rest of the students as a group activity. Encourage them to just simply enjoy the feeling and put down on paper whatever comes to their minds as automatic. They mustn't worry too much about creating the perfect poem. When all groups have their poems ready, ask one volunteer to collect them all and pin them up on the notice board. Leave the poems there for a few days for everyone to enjoy their writing. Alternatively they might find it easier to write Haiku poems.

The Guest House

This being human is a guest house Every morning a new arrival

A joy, a depression, a meanness, some momentary awareness comes as an unexpected visitor.

Welcome and entertain them all! Even if they're a crowd of sorrows who violently sweep your house empty of its furniture

still, treat each guest honourably. He may be clearing you out for some new delight.

The dark thought, the shame, the malice, meet them at the door laughing, and invite them in.

Be grateful for whoever comes, because each has been sent at a guide from beyond.

- Rumi -

31. Top Card

This is a variation of an activity I experienced myself as a participant in Positive Discipline + Training Courses. The group dynamics had an impact on us participants when we happened to find people in our same group with very very similar ways to reacting to things, situations or circumstances. Also to find out qualities that we weren't even a-w-a-r-e of having and recognise them in others. Self awareness helps build up self-esteem and it improves self-regulation. These are key issues in mediation, conflict resolution, and decision making, for instance.

I adapted the same group dynamics to this activity for my students, as a follow-up to a highly interesting Reading task on personality traits from our textbook New English File. The students enjoyed the task when they could find out more about themselves, which often helps when we relate to ourselves and to others.

The exercise is simple and effective. You can limit it to just one stage or add more, depending on how well it works with your group or how motivated you are yourself to facilitate this practice!

STAGE ONE: Have four nice gift boxes ready and some flashcards to fill in each box [flashcards available in www.mindfulenglish.net]. Name each box (1) pleasing, (2) control, (3) comfort and (4) superiority, and place each box in a different corner of the classroom. For example, north – pleasing, south – control, east – comfort, west – superiority. Then invite your students to read the question on the board and take a few minutes to answer the following question to themselves.

Question on the board: what would you say is the most difficult thing for you to put up with: rejection and hassles, criticism and ridicule, stress and pain or meaningless and unimportance.

When they have an answer, ask them to move to their base (north, south, east or west). If the answer is "rejection and hassles" their Top card is (1) Pleasing. If "criticism and ridicule" their Top card is (2) Control. If "stress and pain" Top card is (3) Comfort. If "meaningless and unimportance" Top card is (4) Superiority.

At their base they will find a box with flashcards describing some "Positives" for each Top Card. Ask them to pick up one card each, read the description and express agreement or disagreement to the rest of the people in their small group.

- o - o - o -

STAGE TWO: Remove the "positives" flashcards from the boxes and put in the second set of cards with hints [also available in www.mindfulenglish.net]. Explain to students that if they know a person in the class (or outside) who might fit one of the Top Cards description, today they will be given a little hint to relate to this person more satisfactorily. Perhaps a daughter, a boss, their next door neighbour, or even their husbands or wives! Then invite them to pick up a new card in the box with this piece of information. Allow some time for discussion.

When working with adjectives of personality, I sometimes use the *PD Feeling faces* chart as an add-on [also available in www.mindfulenglish.net].

NB on Mediation

Mediation in Education and other fields is thriving at the moment. An important part of Mediation is based on communicating effectively, relating satisfactorily, and having good social skills. Communicating may be more satisfactory and effective when the parts involved are more aware of themselves, can express how they feel, and respect the same in others.

Adapted from *To know me is to love me* by Lott, L, Matulich K., M and West, D.

32. Woman to woman

This linguistic mediation task to commemorate International Women's Day is presented in two sessions beginning with "48:1" as preparation. When they have completed the previous tasks on 48:1 you can ask your students to finally describe the profile of their ideal female leader [below].

Glued to earlier seasons of The Crown, I very much enjoyed the portrayals of exceptional women in British History displayed throughout the series. Leaving aside the stories of Margaret The Countess of Snowdon and Diana The Princess of Wales, which I personally find sadly fascinating, my main focus today is on the relationship between the first female PM of the United Kingdom and The Sovereign (Netflix The Crown S4:E10).

Female leadership

A lot has been written about the two remarkable personalities being always "at odds". However, my choice is this Netflix performance of the Prime Minister and Queen Elisabeth's last audience [Sequence one 30:34 - 35:25] in order to highlight **fundamental attitudes** such as admiration and mutual respect between women. I am willing to say, first of all, I resonate with many of the words we hear from Mrs Thatcher referring to her Dad's values and principles, which he passed on to her.

For better understanding of this conversation it is highly recommended that the complete episode "War" is watched. Ask your students not to miss Mrs Thatcher's description of the qualities of a good leader [Sequence two 20:03 - 22].

Margaret and Elizabeth

Play Sequence Three [18:15 - 22] with the encounter between Mrs Thatcher and the Queen where a defeated prime minister is shown leaving office after a challenge was launched to her leadership [16:08 - 18:14]. "An act of national self harm" in the PM's words, that puts an end to eleven and a half years of a controversial figure in the United Kingdom. A figure, nonetheless, viewed favourably in historical rankings of British prime ministers.

Shocked by the way Mrs Thatcher left No. 10, Downing Street, Queen Elizabeth calls her in to audience to not only offer her sympathy **from woman to woman** but award the Order of Merit to her **in recognition of exceptionally meritorious service** [Sequence one 30:34 - 35:25]. The order of merit is limited to just 24 recipients no matter their background.

The encounter is representative of a grand gesture overcoming all other failed meetings between the two women. I would like to draw particular attention to the presentation of one woman acknowledging and celebrating one other woman's accomplishments, and focusing on **what they both have in common** instead of the differences that bring the two apart.

To close up this set of activities the first five minutes of episode 48:1 can be played in class "Princess Elizabeth 21st birthday speech from Cape Town". The clip parallels the **fresh start of the two iconic women's careers.**

Do not forget to hold your "round table" and ask for volunteer students to deliver their video lesson practice as proposed in session a "48:1". Eventually complete the profile of their ideal female leader like for instance, accountability, collaboration, cooperation, empathy, integrity, problem solving, or shared vision [sample activity available in www.mindfulenglish.net].

33. Emotional word clouds

When it comes to family and friends students are always willing to talk. Relationships are part of our everyday life, whether at work, in the home, gyms, clubs or neighbourhood there is always this one person you could talk about for hours. And that is so good for speaking activities! Everyone has something to say!!

Here is an adaptation of our textbook Outcomes, and the proposal is to ask students to think of people that would fit into these four categories:

- a family member,
- somebody they get on really well with,
- someone eccentric or unusual or annoying,
- and a person they feel admiration for.

When they have picked someone for each of the categories ask them to write their names on paper (one person on each piece), then put all the names in a jar. Allow some days for them all to think carefully and gradually put names in the jar while you are building up your vocabulary bank with adjectives and expressions to describe people / relationships. You will be able to see how expectation grows until the moment you finally open up the jar and bring one name out, then another, then another... you may wish to ask for one innocent hand to give some assistance in the activity.

As they do students get excited when their teacher is also willing to share some of their life experience, so never hesitate to put in your names as well or even better, should you have the chance, bring a special guest into the classroom as a real life prompt as it was our case. So this very day the lesson begins as usual following normal procedures when very unexpectedly a knock on the door is heard. And it is this stranger whom the teacher starts to talk about and to describe using shaped word clouds projected on the board.

The students eventually started interacting with this "new classmate for the day" as he presented them with riddles and puzzles to solve as well as the most rare adjectives the students will be able to add to their vocabulary banks. Like "objectionable". This was our unforgettable experience.

To create word clouds you can use any of the online resources available on the web. Your students will be delighted to create their own to give away as Birthday cards or Christmas cards for instance.

34. Your position in the family

"Your position in the family" is a multipurpose activity for B1 students to practice speaking skills at the time students learn new personality adjectives. The final result is always quite an impact for everyone as classmates find out they have much more in common than their interest in the language!

THE LESSON

Beginning a new academic year. Just out of the oven textbook New English File. We come across this interesting radio interview [Lesson 1B] about how your position in the family can really tell about your character.

The author: Linda Blair
The book: Birth Order
The content: Personality adjectives

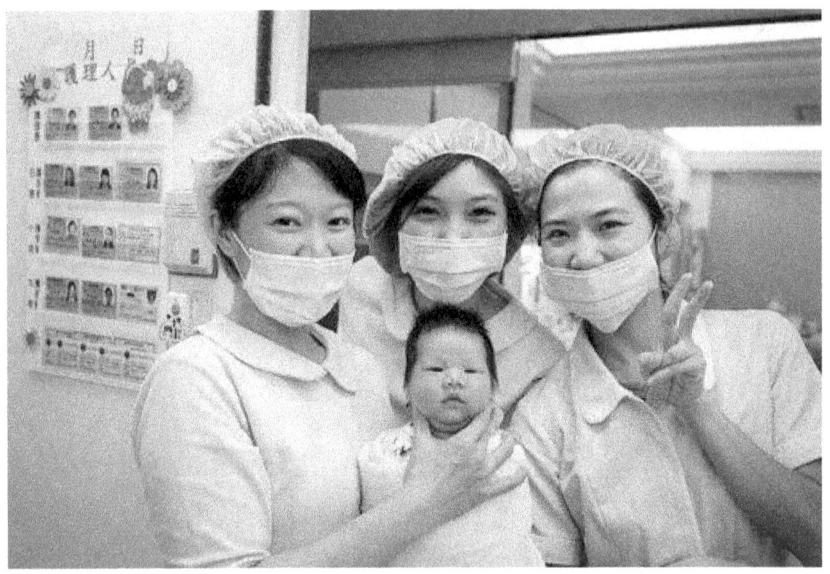

Before listening to the interview I asked students to sit in four different groups following their position in the family: oldest children, middle children, youngest children, and only children. Then listen to the interview in their textbook and pay attention to the adjectives describing each group of children for note-taking.

When a chart has been completed and checked with adjectives of personality for each type of child, they are invited to discuss whether or not they agree with the definitions and give examples. For instance,"I agree with middle children learning to be diplomatic because I very often had to mediate between by eldest sister and my younger ones being a middle child myself" or "I don't agree with oldest children being authoritarian, at least I am not!".

Conversation served up! Students ended up finding out they had had similar anecdotes in their families, which they were happy to share, and similar hobbies and interests which they could discuss for long. We actually also got an idea of the type of persons attending lessons in this group this year. The biggest group was joined by "youngest children" in vast majority. Most shocking of all, as it happens, was finding the only ONLY CHILD in the group sitting at this desk all on his own repeating the words "the story of my life!". Try the dynamics and see what happens... not only does it have quite a visual impact but most important of all "Getting to know each other" during first days at school seems really easy.

With no intention whatsoever to use this to label or stereotype anyone I would like to take the opportunity to expand the topic and introduce this very interesting piece of information I read about Birth Order and Teaching styles which you might like to use to complement the above Listening Comprehension exercise. It has certainly helped me increase my understanding of students and of myself as a teacher, learn methods, and enhance areas that might have been left unknowingly unattended.

A note on birth order and teaching styles

Teachers who are oldest children often like to be in charge. They are often willing to organise interesting and complicated projects for their students. They prefer structure and order and are happiest when students are sitting in neat rows doing as they have been told.

Teachers who are middle children are often as interested in the psychological well- being of their students as they are in academic achievement. They are drawn to the rebellious students and hope to influence them in a more positive direction. These teachers try to achieve order through mutual respect and understanding.

Teachers who are youngest children are often creative and fun- loving and have the easiest time adjusting to noise and disorder. These teachers are often willing to allow students to take more responsibility.

"The significance of Birth Order" from Positive Discipline by Jane Nelsen

35. You've got mail

This is one of the most beautiful Emotional Intelligence practices I have experienced. As a student myself I followed my lecturer's instructions to "open up the envelope at home if you feel so". It is indeed an exciting as well as loving exercise to take every piece of paper out, and read the notes from your classmates.

You can try out this practice with family or friends for more personal circles at special celebrations, for instance. If you choose to get it adapted to your lessons plan you will surely find a topic or task where it fits well. Thanksgiving and Birthdays, or Collocations for a more linguistic objective are good examples. My own choice was to bring the activity as group dynamics for the annual students' representatives Elections as described below.

Hand out empty envelopes for your students to write their names. Ask them to be imaginative and creative as their envelope will be staying on the noticeboard all week for everyone to see. The students will sit in a circle for a few minutes and will be offered crayons, stickers or any useful material you can provide. When they have created their master piece tell them to look at their work for one last time and pass their envelopes to the student on their right who may continue the work. At this point the students will have experienced all kinds of emotions that can be discussed later, when collecting envelopes.

Some minutes later ask the students to give back their envelopes to their classmate sitting to the left. Again they will have different sensations when receiving their original envelope that can also be discussed when the time comes.

The final step at this first stage is for them to hang up all their envelopes somewhere visible all nicely lined up. Leave the envelopes opened and ready to receive messages. This activity works really well in silence and with background music, allowing the students to enjoy watching each other pin up their envelopes and admiring the final result on the noticeboard. Before you go on, they can now share what they experienced during the practice.

To finish up, tell students the envelopes will be staying for one whole week and they are invited to put in "letters" for their classmates [pieces of paper with words or messages]. The content of the letters must be related to these four categories:

gratitude
forgiveness
congratulations
love and kindness

One week later ask the students to go collect their envelopes where classmates have been leaving messages all week and read the messages they have received. The activity can be closed up in a group interaction practice to listen to those willing to share their messages, or their thoughts, feelings and emotions throughout the practice.

The group dynamics can be put into practice as soon as the Students' Representative elections are announced in autumn. All you need is to explain to your group that the envelopes will stay for 15 days or so and will be filled up with good reasons why they believe one person should represent their group at the biannual students representatives meeting.

Their messages will finish the sentence "I believe you could be a good representative for our group" which can be displayed at the top of the envelopes setting. To make a decision they will be quietly paying full attention to their classmates attitudes and behaviours for a fortnight. Here are some of the messages collected in my groups:

You could be a good representative for our group because…

… you are kind and well-spoken

… you talk with confidence

… you were a good representative last year

36. #metime

April 21st 2020: we are living the exceptional circumstances of a global pandemic. We have all been placed on lockdown and must follow our lessons online. The current topic "Every day routines and hobbies" is rather unusual at present, as Life itself is, and here we are at this point of the curriculum learning how to talk about our hobbies and every day lives.

As well as the situation, the students are also exceptional and are adjusting well to new online materials and video conference rooms which replace traditional books and classrooms. Like the saying goes "It is not the strongest of the species that survives, but rather, that which is most adaptable to change".

Throughout lockdown RN [relative normality] has been a priority in this group, and focusing on day-to-day life as we know it. Same times for lessons (now on videoconference rooms), same procedures, same rhythms, same dynamics now combined with new online dynamics. All to try and remain as "normal" as possible in these not so "normal" times that may have been overwhelming for some or most.

So now that this NR [new reality or new normal] is a fact we are ready to move on to the next topic "Talk about your hobbies and free time activities". And asked my A1 students to focus on the 80/20 rule, that is, those activities that bring happiness to our lives and keep us going, considering we are in absolute shutdown. What is that 20% that puts us in a good place to get that 80% of good results for the rest of our day. What are the activities that give Me the oxygen for the rest of the day in confinement.

My #METIME these days is to get up in the morning, and on my own, kindly prepare myself a cup of tea. Enjoy the silence for a short while. Then listen carefully to my favourite radio programme with stories from Quarantine. I just Love listening to "Diario de la cuarentena" at breakfast time. And I focus only on the hot tea that I *feel* and the story that I *hear.* And I breathe in... then out... These fifteen or thirty minutes make my day. It is the 20 that makes my 80.

Can we reinvent ourselves?

How about you? What do you like doing to cope with quarantine? Which of the following activities help you throughout lockdown?

37. The lady with a lamp

What follows is a written Mediation task practicing Translation and Note-taking to commemorate Ms FLORENCE NIGHTINGALE's birthdate on May 12th [resource material available on www.mindfulenglish.net].

INTRODUCTION

You may like to introduce this activity with a reminder of Florence Nightingale, who was born exactly 200 years today.

CONTEXT

The person who is working as an Au-pair to help you at home with the children is somehow confused with the recommendations to follow during Lockdown. You have been asked to translate them into English and after doing some research two texts on how to stay physically and emotionally healthy during the pandemic [available on www.mindfulenglish.net] seemed to best suit the requirements.

The lesson is aimed at beginner Spanish students of English, however, an alternative video is provided so the task can be adapted to higher level groups using information on Easing Lockdown phases, for instance, as well as practising further strategies and techniques like rephrasing, summarising or expanding.

PROCEDURE

If you have time prior to the session, ask students to read the two texts at home and get some examples ready for May 12th lesson. The students are to make sentences recommending **Do's and Don'ts during Lockdown,** for instance, *keep* contact with friends and family like phone calls or videoconferences, or *don't count* the days remaining for the end of the quarantine. They can also make sentences using Can and Can't, for example, *you can't* shake hands or *you can* do sports only at fixed times.

IN CLASS

Play the video clip from the Science Museum [available on www.mindfulenglish.net] and let students take notes on the life of the creator of Rose Chart. Alternative video clips are available too following the life of a nurse at the NHS coronavirus hospitals which were named after the historical character of great relevance at this vital time.

Allow some time for discussion and students' viewpoints, comments, or observations. For example, they might explain why Florence Nightingale was called *the lady with a lamp.* Then, set the students in pairs or small groups to interchange sentences and get them to prepare a final text/map/infographic with recommendations for their English au-pair [approx. 50 words]. They may prefer to record a video or podcast before finally submitting their tasks and that would be good too!

#stayhome #savelives

To top this activity up students were invited to write Thank you notes [below] to their classmate who has been working as a nurse since the state of alarm was declared. Screenshots of the students holding their Thank you notes in their video conference classrooms can be posted on Instagram as a tribute to the many many National Health workers all over the world who stood on the front line to save lives.

For helping your patients
THANK
YOU
and I am proud of people like you

thank you
Thank you, Heroine!

Your devotion and effort is my salvation

thank you!!! .... thank you!!!!.... and thank you!!!!

For your smile every day ❤❤👏👏

For your help and courage
THANK YOU

For all your help!!
thank you!

For giving more than you had!!!
Thank You

For your effort!.
Thank you

For your Unconditional Dedication and Love for Patients
thank you

For exposing your life, to save other lives.
thank
you
Happy Nurses day

Thank You
For your total devotion

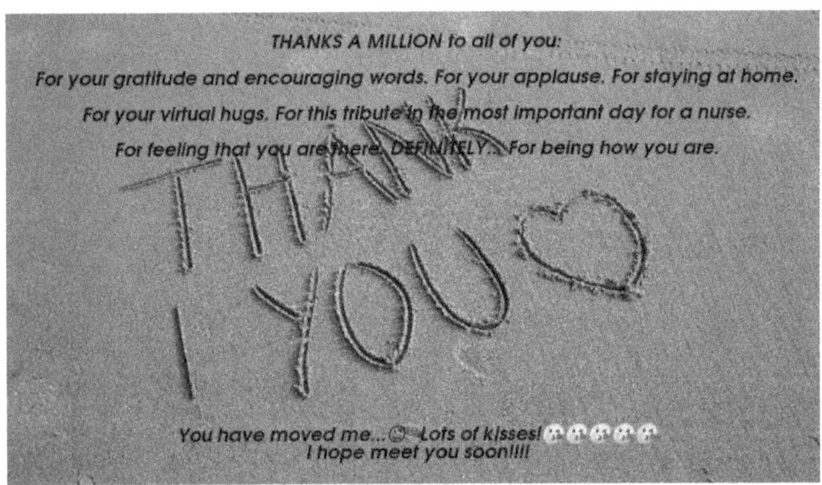
THANKS A MILLION to all of you:
For your gratitude and encouraging words. For your applause. For staying at home.
For your virtual hugs. For this tribute in the most important day for a nurse.
For feeling that you are there. DEFINITELY... For being how you are.
THANK YOU
You have moved me... Lots of kisses!
I hope meet you soon!!!!

38. London Shutdown 1952

C1 EXAM PRACTICE Mediation written task to practice Note-taking.

CONTEXT

A student asks his/her private English tutor for help on a school assignment. He/she has been asked to write an opinion essay based on an international Netflix series from The Crown "Act of God" showing some **parallels** between the **current lockdown** and the **London shutdown** in 1952.

The episode portrays the capital city of the UK impacted by a dense fog, which creates a serious health hazard. Chaos at hospitals, lack of resources and medics, symptoms and dramatic rise in death tolls.As there will be a follow-up written task assigned the students have been asked to focus also on the situations of conflict between the PM and The Queen: language usage samples and conflict resolution practices.

The whole issue puts Churchill's unwillingness to take action in a "vulnerable position" which will be wittingly resolved between the PM and The Queen in the final scenes.

STEPS TO FOLLOW

1. Watch the episode before the lesson. While you watch, take some notes on facts related to the conflict situation: who-what-where-when-why. Examples of similarities between both Shutdowns: SMOG 1952 / COVID 2020. The resolution of the PM's "vulnerable position" by The Queen. Language usage: ways of expressing opinion. Language usage: adjectives to describe conflict (situations or people involved).

2. In- class: watch and discuss the selected scenes [available on www.mindfulenglish.net], then share your notes with your classmates and collaboratively, prepare your "essay drafts" using words and structures to show that you have mastered level C1: Cleft / Inversion / Passive / Conditionals / Participle.

MEDIATION TASKS

– As a mediator, working as the private English tutor by contributing to the student's assignment. Students make it easier for each other to understand all the information on the video by discussing the selected scenes or further research of their interest.

– As an English student, writing an opinion essay of their choice (which actually derived to The PM and The Queen, slides on The Duke of Edinburgh, and TED type of talks on The Clean Air Act!

39. Outdoor activities in Lockdown

Lockdown online bookclub in Nature

It is known by all that the benefits of reading are not only to improve your writing skills and build up vocabulary in L2 but also to *let your imagination fly to other places.* Being at home may not be particularly enjoyable when one has been **locked in confinement** for months. So today's activity is to read, read, read, enjoy travelling to those places even if it is *only* in our imagination, and **get away from Shutdown** a little.

Furthermore, the proposal for our online book club meeting is to be held outdoors in contact with Nature, which is one of the easiest practices within Mindfulness contexts to connect with the present moment. So **our mind is focusing on now,** not on past memories of the pandemic or future plans for a "new normal" kind of life.

One very simple technique to get engaged with present moments is through *the senses*: hear the *sounds* around, feel the *sensations* in the body, or pay close *attention* to what we see. So I would ask all participants to please go find themselves a nice quiet place at home "in the open air" where we can interchange viewpoints and reasons for the liking (or not) of the stories we are reading in lockdown.

They may choose to have their *remote lesson* today by a window in a well lit room, on their terraces or balconies, sitting comfortably near that vase with fresh flowers, or in their favourite little corner where they can get the smells of fresh fruits on the table. Maybe they are the lucky ones with Andalusian patios in the backyard and can hear the sound of fresh water running through a fountain. Or they might simply just sit at the main door steps and feel a fresh breeze. Any place where the five senses can get stimulated... Then enjoy the lesson!

And why invite Mindfulness to our bookclub, by the way? Well, for two reasons basically:

Firstly because cognitive learning skills can be developed through activities in contact with Nature, and

Secondly, you need to come find out!

Here are some of the benefits of Mindfulness in Education:

- bolster student's well-being
- help students thrive academically
- improve overall performance and self-efficacy
- better ability to engage in tasks that require extensive concentration span
- develop focused attention
- learn how to active-listen to others
- time management and work plans
- participants learn how be more present and engaged

Last but not least:

- provide with the skills to rebuild resilience
- decreased frustration
- greater awareness
- increased working memory
- capacity to prevent burnout
- reduced feelings of anxiety and depression
- higher levels of (self) care
- improve distress skills when in stressful situations
- responsible decision making
- anger management and conflict resolution
- participants learn how to recognise and regulate their own emotions and other's
- participants learn how to build up awareness

40. Video conference goodbye

Thinking about a suitable way to close up a very atypical school year which started in the classroom and is coming to an end in a videoconference room.

There are no hands to shake online if you want to say 'Congratulations on a job well done', no eyes to connect when you need to encourage those who couldn't finish up their course. There is no kiss goodbye. No 'Have a well deserved summer time!' hug. No floor to do one last musical chair activity. No tears to comfort and no laughters to join in.

So if you find yourself in my position and feel the inconvenience of closing up this pandemic course in the distance you may like to write a letter to your students. Not only that but also encourage them to write each other a letter, a letter to **a friend** that they made this year which hasn't been other than unique.

After all, it does not happen every year that classmates find themselves locked in their homes for months having to learn by themselves how to download this application to do their tasks. Or find this other platform where they can follow their lessons. It has certainly been weird to follow links to complete synchronous Listening Comprehension activities in real time from home, no matter having to understand how they work first!. As it has been a little nightmare sometimes to get back to the videoconference room when you have been "expelled" several times. But what about trying to listen and repeat to the pronunciation of such word after the teacher when the kids are around!

What an unparalleled end-of-course!

And what good work and strong determination have we all put into getting the course going. I am very positive there are students in the group who, like me, feel an enormous satisfaction to have completed the course in unprecedented times. A person who, like me, will have appreciated collaborative work and team effort, and hours and hours of patiently trying to set it all up in a new reality. And it must have undoubtedly been an extraordinary experience, which has brought us all closer. So here is the proposal for an end-of-course follow-up activity: to write a letter [or email] to that classmate who has become a real friend in adversity this year.

To me it has been a very special year indeed which with difficulty will I be able to forget. I will certainly remember the expressions of uncertainty and preoccupation on the screen every morning, the worries and the questions about the coming weeks, the smiles after lockdown ease, the tears and then the laughters.

I have already written my letter to all of my students. How about you?

June 16th 2020

Dear students,

Nine months ago we met in Classroom 2 on the first floor at EOI Puerta de la Mar. Today we say 'Bye!' on Zoom.
Every school year is different because the students make it special. This year was specially different because a global pandemic changed everything. It isn't the usual thing to close up an English course on a video conference room so I hope this Letter can "replace" a face-to-face last session.

It was a great pleasure to teach English to a class group like yours. Lively and dynamic in the real classroom. Adaptable to videoconference rooms, and happy to try new online applications that were not always user-friendly!!
So congratulations on the efforts, interest and determination you put, especially during these last thirteen weeks in lockdown. It was fantastic to find my students still connecting every morning.
I will always remember my year 2019-2020 pupils. An unforgettable year indeed.

María Teresa Roura Vivas

Acknowledgements

To my Mum and Dad from whom I learned the profession most naturally. To my children from whom I learned *Kindness and Firmness* in Education. To all the pupils that have filled my classrooms every year, who taught me how to better myself and have kept me engaged with long-life learning. To all the professors, colleagues and teachers that inspired me, like Isabel Corrales whose Yoga en el aula motivated this publication. To Margaret and Graham for their selfless assistance.

Bibliography

Adler, A., (1998) Understanding Life, Books.google.com

Ariza, P (2018) Mindfulness en el Centro Escolar María Inmaculada de Sevilla. Retrieved from https://youtu.be/hMzl4BCtHUE

Asunción (2018) Mindfulness en nuestro centro. Retrieved from https://youtu.be/ bG4afMALWlM

Avis, R.P. (2019) Empirically supported benefits of Mindfulness. Retrieved from https://www.apa.org/monitor/2012/07-08/ce-corner

Body, L., Diaz, N. R., Recondo, O., & del Río, M. P. (2016). Desarrollo de la Inteligencia Emocional a través del programa mindfulness para regular emociones (PINEP) en el profesorado. Revista interuniversitaria de formación del profesorado, (87), 47-59.

BBC World news (2013) Mindfulness in Schools. Retrieved from https://youtu.be/ N8M5MJdXvJc

Council of Europe (2001) CEFRL, Common European Framework of Reference for Languages, CUP.

Dellar, H., Walkley, A., (2016) Outcomes Advanced, books.google.es

Doria, J.M., (2012) Meditación transpersonal: 101 claves de meditación y Mindfulness, books.google.es

Dreikurs, R. MD, Soltz, V. (1968) Children: The Challenge, Meredith Press

Gershon, MD. (1998) The Second Brain, HarperCollins Publishers, NY GOV.UK (2019) Mindfulness en 370 centros británicos. Retrieved from https://www.gov.uk/ government/news/one-of-the-largest-mental- health-trials-launches-in-schools

Harper, A (2019) How teachers can help students reduce test anxiety. Retrieved from https://www.educationdive.com/news/how- teachers-can-help-students-reduce-test- anxiety/551507/

Jiménez, Ó (2019) Mindfulness: 6 beneficios inmediatos y Descubre algunos mitos sobre Mindfulness. Retrieved from https:// oliverjjimenez.wordpress.com/

Juslin, P.N. y Vastfjall, D. (2019) Emotional Responses to Music: The need to consider underlying mechanisms. Retrieved from https://www.researchgate.net/publication/23291396_Emotional_Responses_to_Music_The_Need_to_Consider_Underlying_M ec hanisms

Kabat-Zinn, J (2016) Mindfulness para afrontar el estrés y la enfermedad. Retrieved from https://youtu.be/mmdqidh3-N4

Kabat-Zin, J. (2009) Wherever you go, there you are. Hachette Books

Latham-Koenig, C., Oxenden, C., (2019) English File Intermediate, books.google.es Nelsen, J. Ed.D. (2011) Positive Discipline, books.google.com

Menéndez, G (2018) La gestión del estrés a través del Mindfulness en el ámbito educativo. Retrieved from https://drive.google.com/open? id=12aPqqzQ71YMeZZ76jWCpuSgxI_ZKjbhm

Mindful Schools. Retrieved from https://www.mindfulschools.org/

Miller, CJ (2018) Testing a quick mindfulness intervention in the university classroom. Retrieved from https://www.tandfonline.com/doi/abs/10.1080/0309877X.2017.1409345?journalCode=cjfh20&

MiSP (n.d.) Proyecto en Mindfulness para la Educación. Retrieved from https:// mindfulnessinschools.org/mindfulness-in-education/what-is-it/

Naranjo, C. (2005) Cambiar la educacion para cambiar el mundo. books.google.com › books

Peñarrubia, F. (2014) Círculo y Centro, books.google.com

PsicoTools (n.d.) Las mejores universidades apuestan por el Mindfulness contra el estrés. Retrieved from https:// psicologiaymente.com/meditacion/universidades-mindfulness-contra-estres

Publishing Butler, J (2018) When is a time Mindfulness helped you. Retrieved from https://youtu.be/KeVIqgDAP5Y

Ramos, N., Recondo, O., Enriquez, H. (2013) Practica la inteligencia emocional plena, books.google.com

Ramos y Salcido (2017) Programa Inteligencia Emocional Plena aplicando Mindfulness para regular emociones [http://www.lidsen.com/journals/icm/icm-04-01-017#1.2TheMindfulnessandEmotionalIntelligenceProgram(PINEP)] Retrieved from http://ojs.revistadepsicoterapia.com/index.php/rdp/article/view/152

Ramos, N. (2019) The Mindfulness and Emotional Intelligence Program. Retrieved from http://www.lidsen.com/journals/icm/icm-04-01-017#1.2TheMindfulnessandEmotionalIntelligence-Program(PINEP)

Rumi, J. (1995) The Guest House. Retrieved from http://www.rebeccastanwyck.com/Wk4_Handout_Packet.pdf

Santed, MA (2018) Mindfulness: fundamentos y aplicaciones Books.google.com

Sentis Brain Animation Series (2012) Neuroplasticity. Retrieved from https://youtu.be/ELpfYCZa87g

Siegel, DJ. (2007) The Mindful Brain, Books.google.com

Snel, E. (2013) Sitting Still like a Frog, books.google.com

Vollrath, D (2019) Encouraging Students to Develop Resilience. Retrieved from https://www.edutopia.org/article/encouraging-students-develop-resilience

West, D., Lott, L. (2020) To know me is to love me, books.google.com

About the author

María Teresa Victoria Roura Vivas started her career at a very early age in Academia Sta. María del Mar (Fuengirola, Málaga, Spain), as a summer assistant to teachers Mum and Dad. She first began teaching small kids how to read and write in L1, then organised evening English-speaking workshops for young learners when she was only a baccalaureate student. In 1993 she moved to adult education when she became an English teacher for the *Junta de Andalucía* Official Language schools, where she has worked ever since. During her MA studies in Mindfulness and Emotional Intelligence (University of Málaga, 2019) she became powerfully concerned with more **inclusive classrooms** and **well-being** programs at schools. Her other publication "Be Mindful" deals with reducing anxiety and coping with examination stress. At present, she is highly engaged with finding optimal ways to address students with learning difficulties and special needs which is what moved her to launch this publication as fundraising for the cause.

www.ingramcontent.com/pod-product-compliance
Lightning Source LLC
LaVergne TN
LVHW010355160826
845677LV00005BA/1282

* 9 7 8 8 4 1 8 9 1 2 5 7 3 *